**Put Beginning Readers on the Right Track with
ALL ABOARD READING™**

The All Aboard Reading series is especially designed for beginning readers. Written by noted authors and illustrated in full color, these are books that children really want to read—books to excite their imagination, expand their interests, make them laugh, and support their feelings. With fiction and nonfiction stories that are high interest and curriculum-related, All Aboard Reading books offer something for every young reader. And with four different reading levels, the All Aboard Reading series lets you choose which books are most appropriate for your children and their growing abilities.

Picture Readers
Picture Readers have super-simple texts, with many nouns appearing as rebus pictures. At the end of each book are 24 flash cards—on one side is a rebus picture; on the other side is the written-out word.

Station Stop 1
Station Stop 1 books are best for children who have just begun to read. Simple words and big type make these early reading experiences more comfortable. Picture clues help children to figure out the words on the page. Lots of repetition throughout the text helps children to predict the next word or phrase—an essential step in developing word recognition.

Station Stop 2
Station Stop 2 books are written specifically for children who are reading with help. Short sentences make it easier for early readers to understand what they are reading. Simple plots and simple dialogue help children with reading comprehension.

Station Stop 3
Station Stop 3 books are perfect for children who are reading alone. With longer text and harder words, these books appeal to children who have mastered basic reading skills. More complex stories captivate children who are ready for more challenging books.

In addition to All Aboard Reading books, look for All Aboard Math Readers™ (fiction stories that teach math concepts children are learning in school); All Aboard Science Readers™ (nonfiction books that explore the most fascinating science topics in age-appropriate language); All Aboard Poetry Readers™ (funny, rhyming poems for readers of all levels); and All Aboard Mystery Readers™ (puzzling tales where children piece together evidence with the characters).

All Aboard for happy reading!

To my mom, my dad, and my best mate, who believed that I could fly.—J.M.M.

GROSSET & DUNLAP
Published by the Penguin Group
Penguin Group (USA) Inc., 375 Hudson Street, New York, New York 10014, USA
Penguin Group (Canada), 90 Eglinton Avenue East, Suite 700,
Toronto, Ontario M4P 2Y3, Canada
(a division of Pearson Penguin Canada Inc.)
Penguin Books Ltd., 80 Strand, London WC2R 0RL, England
Penguin Group Ireland, 25 St. Stephen's Green, Dublin 2, Ireland
(a division of Penguin Books Ltd.)
Penguin Group (Australia), 250 Camberwell Road,
Camberwell, Victoria 3124, Australia
(a division of Pearson Australia Group Pty. Ltd.)
Penguin Books India Pvt. Ltd., 11 Community Centre, Panchsheel Park,
New Delhi—110 017, India
Penguin Group (NZ), 67 Apollo Drive, Rosedale, North Shore 0632, New Zealand
(a division of Pearson New Zealand Ltd.)
Penguin Books (South Africa) (Pty.) Ltd., 24 Sturdee Avenue,
Rosebank, Johannesburg 2196, South Africa

Penguin Books Ltd., Registered Offices:
80 Strand, London WC2R 0RL, England

Photo credits: cover: Yves Herman/Reuters/Corbis; title page: Yves Herman/Reuters/Corbis; page 5: George McCarthy; pages 6–7: Anup Shah; pages 8–9: Tony Heald; page 10: Paul Hobson; page 11: Pete Oxford; page 12: Nick Garbutt; page 13: Rod Williams; page 14: Arthur Morris/Corbis; page 15: Pete Oxford/National Geographic/Getty Images; pages 16–17: National Geographic/Getty Images; page 19: AFP/Getty Images; page 20: istock.com; page 21: Pete Oxford; page 22: Anup Shah; page 23: Michel Roggo/David Shale; page 24: istock.com; page 25: George McCarthy; pages 26–27: Mike Read; page 29: T.J. Rich; pages 30–31: John Downer; page 33: Anup Shah; pages 34–35: Jose B. Ruiz; page 36: Owen Newman; page 37: Pete Oxford; page 38: Solvin Zankl; page 39: Jose Luis Gomez de Francisco; page 40: Fabio Liverani; pages 42–43: Anup Shah; page 44: Solvin Zankl; page 45: Bruce Davidson; pages 46–47: T.J. Rich; page 48: Pete Oxford.

Library of Congress Control Number: 2008038116

ISBN 978-0-448-45206-7   10 9 8 7 6 5 4 3 2 1

Flamingos

**By Jean M. Malone
with photographs**

Grosset & Dunlap

What is five feet tall?

What has feet with

three webbed toes?

What has a long neck?

Here is a hint—it is a bird

with bright pink feathers!

It is a flamingo!

Flamingos fly just like other birds. They lay eggs like other birds. But they are also different in many ways.

The name *flamingo* comes
from the Latin word *flamma*.
It means "flame."
Long ago, explorers
thought the flamingos'
colorful feathers
looked as bright as fire.

Flamingos have small bodies

and great big wings.

They fly together in long curving lines.
They can fly about 300 miles without
stopping!

A flamingo can balance on one leg.

It tucks the other leg up under its belly.

This helps keep the flamingo warm.

It even sleeps this way!

Does it look as if this flamingo

can bend its knee backward?

It can't, of course!

Its knees are hidden under its feathers.

What you see are the flamingo's ankles!

Flamingos like hot places. They live
in warm, salty lagoons and lakes.
But they need fresh water, too,
for bathing and drinking.

Flamingos spend a lot of time bathing.
But they must keep their
feathers dry for flying.

To keep their feathers waterproof,
flamingos spread oil on their feathers.
The oil comes from a gland near their tail.

There are five different kinds of flamingos. They're called lesser, greater, Chilean, Andean, and puna.

This is a lesser flamingo.
They are about three feet tall.
They are very bright pink.
Most of them live in southern Africa.

Lesser

Puna

The puna, Andean, and Chilean flamingos are a little larger. They live in South America.

Chilean

Andean

The greater flamingo is the largest.
Some are more than five feet tall!
But even greater flamingos don't
weigh much. Most weigh only nine pounds!
That's because they are mostly legs.

Greater flamingos are the only kind
of flamingos that live in the United States.
They live in the Florida Everglades.

The map shows
other parts of the world
where greater flamingos live.

Greater flamingos in North

and South America

are sometimes called

New World flamingos.

They have redder, darker feathers.

Greater flamingos in other

parts of the world

have much paler pink feathers.

Why are flamingos pink?

Why aren't they all the same shade?

The answer is simple:

You are what you eat.

Their food makes them pink!

Flamingos eat foods like shrimp and algae. They both contain lots of carotene (say: kare-uh-teen). Carotene is good for flamingos. The carotene acts like a red dye and turns flamingos' feathers pink.

Lesser flamingos only eat algae.
Greater flamingos eat algae.
They also eat plants, worms,
insects, and shrimp.
A big flock can eat more than one ton
of food in a single day!

Algae

Shrimp

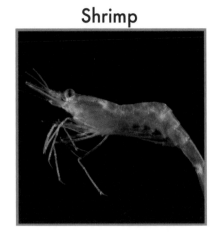

The more carotene a flamingo eats,

the brighter its feathers become.

Flamingos that eat only algae

are very bright pink.

Flamingos that eat algae

and other foods, like shrimp,

are usually a paler pink color.

That's because there is more carotene

in algae than there is in shrimp.

What other foods have carotene?

Carrots and sweet potatoes.

So, could your skin turn pink

like a flamingo

if you eat those foods?

No!

You would have
to eat lots and lots
and lots of those foods every
single day before your skin
would change even a little bit.

Flamingos spend
a lot of time eating.
Even the way they eat
is different from most birds.

The flamingo curves
its long neck all the way around.
Its head is completely upside down
underwater. Then the flamingo
sucks a lot of water into its beak.

Shlurp.
The water contains
a lot of algae.

Inside the beak

are rows of little combs.

They are called lamellae

and act like a strainer.

Tiny hairs on the lamellae

trap the algae.

The flamingo spits out the water

but still has the algae to eat.

Flamingos love to be
around other flamingos!
A group of flamingos
is called a colony.
Thousands—
even a million—
birds might live in a colony.

Flamingos do everything together.

They eat and sleep together.

They even mate at the same time.

Flamingos spend lots of time

talking to each other.

They *SQUAWK, GRUNT,*

HONK, and *CLICK* their bills.

What does all of this talking mean?

No one knows for sure!

Before flamingos mate,

they put on long, fancy shows.

The whole colony dances together!

They march, twist, stretch, and wave.

The females say *EEP, EEP*.

The males reply *CAK, CAK*.

Here is something amazing.

Flamingos won't mate unless

everything is perfect for raising chicks.

Before mating, they check to make sure

that there is plenty of food

and that the weather is warm enough.

Soon it's time for the female to lay her egg. The male and female build a nest near the water that looks like high, round mud hills.

Each female lays only one white egg.

It looks like a chicken egg.

The female and male take turns

sitting on the egg for about thirty days.

Then, the chick hatches.

Baby flamingos have soft gray or white feathers. Their parents feed them a dark red liquid. It is called "crop milk." It is full of carotene. The parents feed their chick until it can fly.

After about two weeks, a chick can walk
and swim. Then it joins all of the other
chicks in a crèche (say: kreh-sh).
The crèche is like flamingo day care.
A crèche can have as many as 30,000
chicks in it. A few adult flamingos guard
the crèche at all times.

After ten weeks,

flamingo chicks

begin to fly!

They get a running start

on their long, skinny pink legs,

then they take off into the sky.

They are as big as

their parents by age two.

Now the chicks have new
brown and gray feathers.
They will have grown-up
pink feathers when they
are about four years old.

Once the flamingos turn pink,
they are ready to join in the dancing.
They are ready to start flamingo
families of their own.

In the wild, flamingos
can live for thirty or forty years.
They usually mate twice a year.

Flamingos do have enemies.
Jackals and foxes hunt flamingos.
Big birds like eagles will also eat
flamingos and their eggs.

In some parts of the world,

people steal flamingo eggs, too.

They eat the eggs as a special treat.

The puna flamingos were

almost wiped out because

so many of their eggs were stolen.

Not so long ago,

hunters killed almost all

the North American flamingos.

They wanted pink feathers

to put in fancy hats!

Today, there are laws
against hunting flamingos.
And flamingo homes
are better protected.
Flamingos are safer.

Flamingos still need our help.

Pollution and climate change

can hurt flamingos.

Pollution can make lakes

too dirty for flamingos.

It can also destroy the algae

that flamingos eat.

Recycling,

turning out lights,

and not wasting water

are all things you can do

to help make sure

flamingos are safe.